Sharron Taylor

IN SEARCH OF LOVE

Content Warning

This book contains references to childhood trauma,
sexual abuse, physical violence, suicide, self-harm,
and emotional distress.
These topics are presented with honesty and
vulnerability, not for shock, but for healing—and
in the hope that others feel less alone.
Reader discretion is advised, especially for those
in the early stages of their healing journey.
If you are currently struggling, please consider seeking
support from a trusted mental health professional or
crisis resource in your area. You are not alone.

"Let us not love with words or speech but with actions and in truth."
— *1 John 3:18 (NIV)*

"When my heart is overwhelmed, lead me to the rock that is higher than I."
— *Psalm 61:2*

"You are your best thing."
— *Toni Morrison*, from Beloved

Contents

Prologue

All my life I've had to fight.
All my life I've been a wife.
Reflecting on my childhood God was preparing me.

I am equipped with the strength to raise a family.
I am trained to love through pain.
I am rewarded with the magic that happens in my brain.

I AM love!
I AM peace!
I AM everything God planned for me to be!

I started writing poetry when I was about fourteen—
Not for praise, but for healing.
Writing became my release, my way to make sense of pain
and find purpose through it.
This book is a reflection of that journey.
A collection of real-life encounters, heartbreaks,
lessons, and prayers.
It's titled *In Search of Love* because that's
what I've been doing all along—
Searching for love from parents, from friends, from siblings,
And holding onto the hope of one day finding a partner
who could love me the way God says love should be.

Part I:

Broken Foundations

*This section begins where the pain began—childhood.
These poems confront generational trauma,
abandonment, abuse, and the quiet ache of growing
up without protection. It's a raw look at how early
wounds shape us, but also how naming them
is the first step to healing.*

Breathe

How dare you tell your secrets to me,
You lay the burdens of your troubles down on me.
Secrets so, dark they bare weight,
Made in the absence of light birth hate.
Breathe.
This was a lot to handle,
Just mere pieces of a true scandal.
But it was meant for me,
Because she's always been weak.
She needed me to carry this for her; she couldn't take it anymore.
Deadweight on broken pieces couldn't hold any more.
Breathe.
She is the product of abandonment
Never had a daddy, mommy could never quite handle it.
A motherless child,
She was gone by fifteen, somehow, she had to figure it out.
She was a victim of molestation,
She was 5, 6, 7, 8, 9, 10.
She never quite healed, it became her foundation.
Breathe.
For 12 years she was the product of physical abuse
Called himself a husband and a father, he beat the children too.
One upside down, one till he bled, they were both two.
I'd prepare for frequent seizures from how he beat my mother blue.
Somehow, I wished we were blood so that he would beat me too.
Breathe.
She is the product of sexual abuse
Mostly to blame alcohol and drug use.
She said she never wanted to be the cause of it
But anytime she was high she'd let anyone in.
I remember very vividly of that man's hands on my skin.

Or the other time when I was at mommy two's
For the three nights straight, my uncle gave me the blues
Breathe.
She held hands with suicide as she began to believe
that she was weak.
She nearly gave in to the defeat.
She is the product of depression,
The product of aggression.
The product of a woman who was a master at digression.
The product of a stigma she was determined to beat
Breathe.
She is the product of incest,
A secret I cannot tell yet.
A product of neglect.
A product of a weak woman who tried her best.
A product of illusion, no one really knows what to believe,
A product of confusion, she can't wait to leave.
The past behind her and sail different seas.
Breathe.
I am She and She is me.
She is strong and relentless
Driven and independent
God fearing and ambitious
Powerful and consistent
She is humble and original
Adaptable and dependable
Breathe.
She is everything they thought she couldn't amount to be.

Mystified

Who am I and what am I doing?
I have no VALUE: Voice, Ambition, Love,
Understanding, and Emotions.
I have no reason for living and devotion.
In love with the HARD: Hate, Anger, Rage, and Death.
I have no self-respect or good health
Ignorant to the CARE: Companionship, Affection,
Respect, and Ecstasy from my family
Twinged by the HURT: Heat, Unveil, Rampage, and Threat.
Constantly breaking into deep sweat.
Detrimented by FEELINGS: Future, Emotions, Embarrassment,
Lust, Incredulous, Needs, Greed and
Sorrow.
Not having my own constantly have to borrow
Dying slowly from DRUGS: Denial, Refrain, Uneasiness,
Guilt, and Subsist.
Live not by the sword or the fist.

Suicide

She slept all night after she cried all night.
Woke up and she still had sleep in her eyes.
So, she went to the bathroom to wash her face.
She said to herself today would be the last day.
She was going to change her future and let the past be the past.
Promised herself that last night's cry would be her last.
So, she put on her makeup.
Just to cover up.
The pain in her face.
That remained from yesterday.
So, it wouldn't come off, she put on her lipstick twice.
Did he hair up real nice.
She put on a pretty, long black dress and a leopard print stiletto.
She started to think about the betterment of tomorrow.
She put on her perfume and headed to the car.
She drove till the night was lit from the stars.
She went in the glove box and soon after went to sleep.
Along with a letter she wrote,
she put her wallet on the seat, and it read,
I cried till I could cry no more.
I tried till I could try no more.
I loved till I saw that love don't love back.
Somehow, I couldn't learn to live with that.
Here is all my money and everything I've earned.
Live life in remembrance of me and everything that you've learned.
And may God have Mercy!!

Take Me

Tired of being hated
Misunderstood and unappreciated.
It feels like I am losing everything I got.
I thought I was doing right, it turns out I'm not.
No more sad sobbing and sighing.
This will be my last time crying.
No more sister and I'm losing the next thing
close to me, my best friend.
My only friendship may be coming to an end.
I hate feeling this way.
The pain may end on day.
Sometimes I'm tired of living; ready to die.
My only question about stress and depression is why?
Why me?
Is this the way life must be?
Because I walk with God this is my trial.
Waiting patiently till the next time I smiled.
My feelings are farther than skin deep they're real.
I hate it all, but this is how I feel.
Beauty is only skin deep and it's not looking too good inside.
I have many feelings I can no longer hide.
Having no father is more than hurt it's painful.
No need to feel doleful.
Having no one to express my feelings to,
don't think anyone would care.
Feeling so lonely with anger, I don't want to lose the only thing
that's there. Don't want to lose what might be here for a while.
The one boy who makes me smile.
I hope he ain't all about game.
If he is, in the end I won't be the same.

I hate flesh and feelings. So many cuts, scrapes,
bruises, and mixed emotions.
Tired of listening to lies about life, love and devotion
Dear God do a favor for me.
Take love,
Take evil,
Take emotions,
Take pain,
Take flesh,
Or take me.

Tears of Pain

What caresses my face?
Gentle, slinging down glazing my lips.
I feel sexual frustration when you're caressing my hips.
Hormones fill my body with rage
I feel you looking at me with a sexual gaze.
I love the feeling of just us.
Your eyes filled with love but more lust

What caresses my face?
Cracked out and yet controlling it fills your body with pain.
One more problem on my plate, hate is what I gain.
I want... No, I need you to know that I love you.
It's not that I hate you, it's the things that you do.
You see the pain in my face, your expression in wow.
You're not sure of what I am feeling so your question in how.

What caresses my face?
I have little family, so I don't want to lose you.
I don't want to stress or mentally abuse you.
We're sisters and yet still best friends.
I'll be there for you all the way to the end.

What caresses my face?
Thoughts that everything around me changing.
Everyone's growing up, we're quickly aging.
I want you to be in my life.
You are the husband, and I am the wife.
I pray night after night that you don't lie and despise me.
I believe that you love me so you will never deny me.

What caresses my face?
Soft vices of evil try to intrude my temple.
I know it's not God so it's very simple.
He wants me to feel suicidal.
I have three strong people who I see as idols.
I don't want to lose you, but changes are still here.
Losing everyone I love is my only fear.

What caresses my face?
Tears of Pain!

Unborn

Born into sin and I am tired of living
Never born have no worries
Never born have so many stories
Never born have no lies
Never born no need to cry
Never born have so many tears
Never born have so many fears
Never born have no heartache
Never born no more heartbreaks
Never born there would be no envy
Never born there would be no me
Never born no worries of lost friends
Never born have to worry about sin
Never born I would be God's child
Never born no need to ask why or how
Never born have no family
Never born never lonely
Never born no pain
Never born have nothing to gain

Driving Thoughts

Driving on the way to school, in my mind,
in my car, I just though.........
It's not that I'm losing my faith or losing any trust
It's just,
Faith without action is dead and I'm afraid I'm not doing enough.
My people who I motivate say, "girl I think you doing too much"
They say you never know who your strength will touch,
You never know how your strength is teaching
And how your faith is preaching
Or who your courage is reaching
I pic my head up just a little, but it's still not enough
I tell myself I must be stronger cause he said
he'd never give me too much

Part II:

Searching for Something Real

Here, the search for love begins. These poems trace the emotional rollercoaster of wanting to be seen, chosen, and cherished. Through vulnerability and heartbreak, they reveal the complexities of relationships, the cost of misplaced hope, and the yearning for something authentic.

Bittersweet

I lay in bed tears caress my face.
I imagine being in my happy place.
Only my happy place was with you and you took that.
I try to move forward but you stay in my rearview and I look back.
I look back so often hoping that things would change.
Knowing you could love me and you could give me your name.
But he's afraid of change or he's just afraid to change.
I'm afraid he's making a mistake.
I'm afraid to feel my heart break.
See I don't think I know what love is.
I never been loved back from the love that I give.
With you, I can't quite tell what I'm feeling.
My hearts been broken and I know I'm still healing.
But you bring something different, I love the way you make me laugh.
I can be myself the way I never have

Choose

Put your ear to my heart and hear it crack
If you'll lie once, you'll lie twice and that's that
Want it to work but you ain't doing your part.
Gotta get to the end but first we need a good start,-.
I love you so much and you don't hear me.
I love you but I can't handle you lying to me.
Don't want to stop you from doing what you do.
If you don't want to be with me then that's on you.
Not to open my heart is what you're teaching so I learn.
Keeping my heart closed because I am tired of turns.
Turns that flip my heart the wrong way
I'll want to believe you truly love me one day.
But when you're through and you're tired, know that I loved you.
And you never love or care for me then do what you do.

Fake Friends

I close my eyes, and I can still feel what it feels like to be close to you.
I feel your toes pressed against mine and I'm standing in front of you.
I can feel your hand as it slowly caresses my face,
as if it were the first time.
Four fingers on the back of my neck, thumb right in front of my ear,
I feel your touch in my spine.
Long time, if at all I can say I ever felt like this.
On my forehead, you planted a kiss.
A kiss, that went so far down in my heart it touched my soul.
This is the first time I've stood next to a man and felt whole.
I feel you look into my eyes like you've seen me before.
Or perhaps, as if you never wanted to let me go.
No words were spoken, with every touch said you'd
protect me and I should give you my heart.
That I did and I was all yours and although
you weren't mine it was a start.
I can feel your arms wrapping around my body,
I've never been held so tight.
As your chest touched mine I could hear your body say,
relax, it's alright.
John 3:18 let us not love in word or talk but indeed and in truth.
I could only listen to what your actions made me do.
Your breath on the side of my face it was warm to feel.
Every vibe I got from you I took and it was real.
I prayed many nights and I have never been so sure.
I had gone without for so long and you were my cure.
I am for you and you are for me is truly what I believe.
But then you open your mouth and with your words you deceive.
You would lie and each word you spoke cut me so deep.
I feel me internally bleeding, I pray my spirit won't die.

Night after night the only way to sleep is to cry.
I tried to fight it and you see the love I have for you is true.
In each fight this love wins every time.
You have infected my mind.
You have infested my life and everything comes
with a memory of you.
Whether I am awake or asleep or with anything that I do.
I trusted you with my heart, only for you to throw it out.
I gave you love to be loved back with no doubt.
In this moment, I learn that love is stronger than hate
with so many reasons to hate you.
Yet I can only miss you and still love you,
though I must have mistaken you.
One day he'll mend my heart, and I will pick my head up again.
And maybe one day I'll have the opportunity
to fall in love with a real friend.

I Imagine

I've imagined us hand in hand exchanging vows and I do's
I've imagined you on top of me and me on top of you.
I've imagined bearing your children.
I've even imagined your seeds as twins.
I've imagined us cap and gown, hand in hand.
I've imagined us laying up on beaches of jet black sand.
I've imagined that every smile I made was because of you.
I've imagined a million ways to show you I love you.
I've imagined you trusting me with your life.
I've imagined you wanting me to be your wife.
But this makes the difference between imagination and real life.
Because in real life, he was afraid of commitment.
Loving me exceeds the limit.
Making him happy is only a figment,
Of our imagination, he's indifferent
About the way I make him feel and
My love is consistent.
But he's so resistant.
And still so inconsistent.
But I'm still persistent.
And insistent.
All I want is to live how it's written.

I Want

How I sit back and create a bucket list of simple shit
I think my man should be able to give me with a quickness.
Like the feeling of his hands on my thigh,
When we ride.
Or the kiss on my forehead when he kisses me goodbye.
I want to look into his eyes
And see how he sees me as the mother of his children
and forever his wife.
I want a man who can take everything I have to offer.
And in return love me harder.
Baby let me be your weakness and in return you be my strength.
See I know this is what God meant.
I just want to love him and put nothing but God above him.

You

You go me over here craving your body, craving your lips on mine.
How you...... touch me on the inside.
Craving your....um,
And the way your fingertips,
Caress the small of my back.
Damn, I want that.
Right now when I'm missin you.
Can only reminisce about kissin you.
Laying next to you no worries.
We can do this all day in no hurry.
We aint rushin into nothin.
Cause when the time come he gone love how I love him.
And I want him.
I want him like a fat kid love cake.
The way they want double rice and yum yum sauce on a plate.
I tell myself age don't matter when it do.
You don't want me the way I'm wanting you.
Feeling like I need you.
I fuckin hate it when I see you.
I'm beginning to be see through.
I be, fighting myself saying fuck him.
Then again, I want to fuck him.
And again, I want to love him.
Shaking my head, then again, fuck him.
The joy I get from him erases the pain away.
The sex I get from erases the day away.
It's so time consuming.
And he's so mind consuming.
It's selfish how he takes up all the space in my head.

In My Head

He excites me,
Real life Jill Scott ignites me.
It seems so soon,
How we make plans to jump the broom.
Outside looking in it looks premature.
He thinks I'm a blessing I'm not sure if he's sure.
They're looking at us crazy
But we both been waiting,
And he's been patient, but he's been hurt n I want to heal him,
Reveal to him, my intentions. I want to love him,
Put only God above him,
I stopped waiting and he came through like a thief in the night.
Inside he found the light.
He lit me up and it was magic,
How we dropped our hoes was tragic.
Nothing else mattered but how he saw the future in me.
How he saw a future with me
How we could grow and sow seeds,
How we would one-day exchange rings,
It doesn't really roll off his tongue and it isn't easy to say
But I'm like a dream come true from that night that he prayed.
And he is everything I couldn't imagine.
Embodied with perfection.
He resembles me,
Like Adam and Eve.
I am the queen to his king,
He is the words when I sing,
I am the band to his ring,
He is the rock that I have been,
I know he's heaven sent.
Just give me your whole heart and with it ill protect.

To his eye, I was like the sun set,
Embodying the beauty of a goddess,
With a humble heart and quite modest.
A familiar feeling takes over as I get chills down my spine.
I want to make him mine,
But I need him to want me the same,
Love me with no shame,
Willing to change my name,
This is insane,
I would be foolish to pump the breaks on a blessing,
I want to be loved with no question,
I want to give him everything he's been missing,
Love him with no limit.

Love Me Longer

You light a fire inside me that I would like to call passion.
You left love inside me that I know was nothing less than magic.
You ignite me.
Do nothing less than excite me.
He gives me hope that we are destined.
I don't question him for a second.
He has sent nothing less than a blessing'.
Though like a plague he has infected
My mind
And in the beginning, it was simple our love was divine.
And together we lose track of time
I can't help but to want to make you mine.
I fell in love with what was on the inside.
And I pray you push that demon out the way.
Before he sends you astray.
And you might lose me.
How could you hold your blessing so loosely?
As if you too, weren't afraid to lose me.
Just promise that when you stop listening to that voice in your head
That one that says, "it's okay, go ahead,
Love her,
Trust her,
Put only me above her."
That you won't apologize for loving me,
only that you wouldn't love me longer.

Part III:

Falling, Failing, and Feeling

This is the messy middle. Love arrives but doesn't always stay. Passion and disappointment blur the lines as infatuation, loss, and lessons intertwine. These poems explore how loving others often forces us to face the parts of ourselves we've neglected.

Mr. Smith

I didn't know much about him but his sign.
That he was fine,
And I wouldn't mind,
Having his body near mine.
I met him, and he met me, but more on an intellectual level;
I like his mind.
The things we could accomplish if our minds combined.
If I'm being honest, he makes me aware of my insecurities.
He makes me want to be a better me.
Reminds me of my strengths and that only love makes me weak.
He makes me think.
As if I don't think enough already.
He's on my mind heavy, I can't say why.
I've even seen him in my dreams.
He seems to only come to me in my sleep.
But I ain't trippin, I'm intrigued.
The way superstition has it, he was thinking of me.
He makes me want to get to know him.

Persistence

Each chance I get to meet him I want to learn him,
He seems like the type to fall in love with I want to earn him,
God fearing above all things
A father who takes the time to pay attention to the simple things,
I mean,
I think I've seen mirages of someone like this in my dreams,
He wears his confidence like clothes,
He knows that's attractive I suppose,
He's connected through emotion,
Sometimes he ashy and needs lotion,
I'm joking,
See he's a comedian and I thought if he read that he would laugh,
I wrote this poem on my behalf,
Cause I be thinking,
26 and an ex-husband
Did she ask for too much, or nothin,
I'm buggin, f*k it
He has a strong desire for success,
I hope he accepts nothing less,
Self-aware and pays attention,
Oh, and did I mention,
I think he's gifted,
The way he has a way with his words and
the potential to keep my lifted,
See I don't think you get it,
He seems so perfect,
In world where almost everything seems unworthy
Though he seems like a figment of my imagination,
He likes to all me temptation,
He's persistence,
With eyes made to see me at a distance.

Reminiscin

Jazz was my first love and ik his love was true.
He loved me, never judged me.
My hats off to you.
To the fathers of my children, I won't name.
Both you niggas lame.
You won't get no fame off me.
Both of you dead to me.
Rest in peace, rest in peace.
Kenny #1 was a real one.
This love I'm pretty sure I never healed from.
Loved me so much I learned to love me.
You struggled wishing that other hoe was me.
Mike you my nigga guess we was meant to be friends
Taught me the base standards and what a gentlemen is.
Justin was my bae our life was different.
Bae was ambitious, showed me a different life
and exposed me to how I wanna be livin.
My favorite time was when I met you in Cali
We drove to Vegas just cause Cali was raining.
Swear that was almost my favorite vacation.
I locked you in as Kenny name you were my Kenny #2
I never gave you a chance cause I know I wasn't really right for you.
You and I were too different.
You deserve somebody with whom you could share interest.
Kenny #3 you were special to me.
I still watch you on the gram wondering what if for you and me.
I think about you every time I get close to collard greens.
Will they gone read and wonder if its true.
You still my best kept secret and they gone wonder if its you.
I won't forget the night you saved me and you
put me on to Snowfall in ya room.

Jordian you reminded me that I was capable of loving
It had been a few years and I was afraid that I wasn't.
That was short lived cause we had two different agendas.
Alpi was special we met over seas.
We met on a boat ride somewhere in turkey in the sea.
The whole thing was surreal it still feels like a dream.
The way he looked at me and said, "mashallah"
was like nothing I could dream.
Alpi I fuckin hate you cause you lied to me.
Izzy I met you just a few years before this
You was fine and ambitious and I hoped that we would stick.
You rescued me in Mexico and we spent some time in Texas.
That time and your touch was most definitely infectious.
Every time we link its like I've known you forever.
Always a pleasure every time we're together.
The vibe just natural we ain't forcing nothin.
Feeling like a kid again how you be having me blushin.
Twenty twenty two im still single but I aint trippin.
Just reflecting on my memories, you can call it reminiscin.

Love Me Like

Love me like God so loved the world, he gave his only begotten son.
Love me like you've craved to love me like I was the one.
Love me like you've waited lonely nights for this kind of love.
Love me right and hold me tight so we will never lose this love.

Infatuation

Initiated with infatuation, how I adore studying you.
Tempted to declare, I despair the thought of me being with you.
We had a sexual attraction.
Which was our body's natural reaction.
An unexplainable chemistry that led our desire to passion.
As I acquire of your pride to be a man, I decide
you should let me be your woman.
I'll show you prominent devotion.
My love will only be a fourth of my emotion.
This is my confession.
Of a diminutive obsession.
I bestow upon you my eminent affection.
I hope that your perception of me,
Is what I think we might be destined to be.
This is more of a blessing than luck.
I hope you find it in your core to lend me your trust.

With You

I lay in bed tears caress my face
I imagine being in my happy place
Only my happiness once lied with you and you took that
I try to look forward, but you stay in my rear view and I look back
I look back so often hoping things will change
Knowing you could love me and give me your name
But he is afraid of change
Or maybe he is afraid to change
I'm afraid he's making a mistake
I'm afraid for my heart to break
See I don't think I know what love is
I've never been loved back from the love that I give
With you I can't quite tell what I'm feeling
My heart has been broken and I know I'm still healing
But you bring something different
I love the way you make me laugh
I can be myself the way I never have

Part IV:

Becoming

In this section, the healing begins to take root. Through spiritual clarity, emotional maturity, and self-recognition, these poems shift the focus from brokenness to becoming. They mark a turning point: the realization that love starts within, and peace must be chosen.

Know My Worth

A man will be something till he's nothin
Thought he said he loved me, he was frontin
Guess that ring on my finger don't mean nothin
Thought it was love we just f*ckin
So, listen to me clear and run back and tell him
That I tried my damn hardest, but I refuse to settle
I been in it for the long hall and I'm losin
I know I'm a winner so I refuse to do this
We ain't getting married cause I'll be damned if I'm stupid.

Love Not Mine

I ain't never been in love like this.
I ain't never had no drug like this.
And I'm addicted to his love, his touch.
I ain't never needed something so much.
He is my oxygen the way he gives me life.
He is my way out of the dark the way that he shines so bright.
He is my strength when I feel weak.
He is the wind beneath my wings.
He is my color when the skies are gray.
He is the smile upon my face.
He is my comfort place.
My escape.
To my pain he brings ease.
And in the madness he brings me peace.
He is my peace of mind.
Supports me better than my spine.
How was he not made to be mine.

Confusion

I hate the confusion I'm feeling
I assume it's all a part of the process of healing.
I never knew what it felt like to be broken
But I'm broken,
Afraid that I'm damaged. I sit back and try to wait on God.
I do what they say and work on me.
Continue to be strong and find ways to strengthen my weak.
But I'm weak.
I just want to love and to be loved, what is wrong with me.

Lightskin Twin

I had to go to tinder,
to remember how he first got my attention
He was tall and handsome, looked like he had some business
Let me not fail to mention
he was sexy as hell and his body caught my eye
So, I decided to swipe right
And then -- I waited
I waited just a short time,
To find that I too had caught his eye
I wasn't trippin, but listen
The conversation from beginning,
Had captured my undivided attention
He pointed out the way I stand out
And how I be lookin different
This match was nothing less than significant
Found out he was my lightskin twin and shi*
And only after a few days I am feeling quite ambivalent
He was like a 6 foot 5 sexy ass stimulant
The way he stimulated my dreams, goals, body and mind
Damn, I hope one day he might consider being mine
But in the meantime
I hope to simply maximize our time
I want to give him all of me
Pour back into him what he's already poured into me
A friendship that could be infinite
A possibility of a love that could only be described as innocent
Everything about him felt genuine
Time with him made me see things different
But like all thing this too had ended quick

Part V:

A Heart That Still Hopes

Though the road has been rough, hope remains. These closing poems are a quiet prayer—for closure, for connection, and for the kind of love that doesn't ask you to shrink. This section is a soft landing, a celebration of resilience, and a reminder that healing is never the end—just a new beginning.

Desire

It has been a while since I've been able to find the words but,
Lately my heart is inspired.
The longer I sit with myself the more I understand of my desires.
I desire to love and to be loved completely.
I want to find the body to these ribs who completes me.
I desire to find the one who asked God for me.
Who prayed for the best in me specifically.
Anticipating the moment God favors you with me it's the moment
we've been waiting for.
I desire to be prayer for.
I desire to be led.
I Want my spirit to be fed.
I desire to be held tight, loved right, and kept warm at night.
I desire romance.
Someone like me who shows love at every chance.
I desire life.
I desire not to simply find a husband, but I pray I'll be a wife.
I am definitely the type.
I grow everything I am given.
I will turn our house into a home.
I desire to find true love, because of me I know it exists.
The kind of love that will persist.
The kind of love that never quits.
I desire to love with my mind, body, and spirit.
I want to give the kind of love that is healing.
I want my love to be new.
I want my love to heal your wounds.
I desire to be your safe space, the one you chose to vent to.
I desire to indulge in reciprocity.
Feeling comfort in loving you the way that you are loving me.

I look forward to mastering the art of loving you
1 million and more ways.
I desire to love just one person for the rest of my days.
I don't think I am asking for much. I just want to give you me.
I have been waiting so patiently.
I just want to be your peace.
I desire to be your only and to never have to compete.
I desire to feel safe in his presence knowing he will go to war for me.
I desire intentionality, show me that I'm your priority.
I desire love and loyalty.

Counting My Blessings

Dear God, I want to thank you in advance.
I have a strong feeling that you have sent me my man.
You know, the one you made me for.
Pretty sure I have his rib.
It's no wonder the only place I want to be is in his skin.
He is perfect.
I know he knows that I am worth it.
We're moving genuinely but it's fast.
Scared out of my mind because I want this to last.
Feels too good to be true.
Still somehow, I think he was sent by you.
He is handsome, I love his face.
I love the way he is always in my space.
The way he holds me I feel safe.
I wanna learn him so I can love him different.
I want my love to be infinite.
I wanna heal his wounds and be his safe place.
I will love him for the rest of my days.
I wanna learn and love them first all of his insecurities.
I wanna take care of his heart and put his mind at ease.
Dear God, let me be his peace.
I love the way he handles me.
When I'm in a mood he has patience.
He eases all of my frustrations.
He pays attention to the little things and those
have always mattered most.
He knows everything I need because he is always taking notes.
I know he has some growing, but I love him right where he's at;
I wouldn't change a thing.
I pray we always grow together and that we want the same things.
I think about his daily.

He might be the love of my life and I want to carry his babies.
I wanna give him the best of me.
I just want to make him happy.
I love to see him smile and that gap between his teeth.
I need to see him every day of the week.
I love the way his presence comforts me.
I pray I never give him a reason to leave.
I love the way our love is not familiar, it is new.
I never want to remember what my life was like without you.
I love the way he is intentional; I want him to know I see him.
I see him doing whatever it takes, even if it takes time.
Sometimes I need the reassurance that I am his and he is mine.
I want him all the time.
Dear God, as the days add up I feel the enemy creeping.
Constantly at my mind trying his hardest to defeat me.
I question,
Is this God sent or a distraction?
Calm my mind from the noise.
I would like to clearly hear your voice.
God, please lead me.
I know even though he's still growing he completes me.
Lord keep me.
Matter of a fact, keep WE.
May you encourage us to never have cold feet.
And may all our choices be easy.
I pray his good always outweighs his bad.
I pray I'm good for him in ways he's never had.
I prcay we never keep secrets.
And that our giving to one another remains frequent.
Thank you for him and his heart, I promise I will protect it.
I promise to always see the good in him and always count our blessins.

Call to Action

If this book resonated with you—if you saw pieces of your own story reflected in mine—I invite you to share it.

Tell your story. Write your truth. Speak the words you were once afraid to say. Because healing doesn't just happen in silence. It happens in community, in connection, in courage.

You can connect with me on social media or by email. Let's keep the conversation going. Let's keep choosing healing—every single day.

And if you know someone who needs to know they're not alone, pass this book along.

Because love—real love—starts with understanding.

Epilogue

I used to think healing meant pretending things didn't happen. That strength was silence, and survival was enough.

But I've learned that true healing means facing it—unpacking the truth, saying it out loud, grieving it, forgiving where you can, and walking away when you must.

This book holds everything I thought would break me. And yet, here I am. Still standing. Still writing. Still growing. Still searching—but no longer desperate. I've learned that love isn't something I need to chase. It's something I can build, from within.

So, wherever you are in your story, I hope you choose to turn the page. Even when it's hard. Especially when it's hard. Healing isn't linear, and peace isn't passive. But it's possible. And you deserve it.

Thank you for walking with me.

Acknowledgements

Because love—real love—starts with understanding. And if you know someone who needs to know they're not alone, pass this book along.

You can connect with me on social media or by email. Let's keep the conversation going. Let's keep choosing healing—every single day.

Tell your story. Write your truth. Speak the words you were once afraid to say. Because healing doesn't just happen in silence. It happens in community, in connection, in courage.

If this book resonated with you—if you saw pieces of your own story reflected in mine—I invite you to share it.

About the Author

Sharron Taylor is a mother, Army veteran, college graduate, and survivor whose journey from trauma to triumph is as inspiring as it is unflinching. Born in Illinois and raised in Atlanta, she has overcome homelessness, abuse, addiction in the family, and single motherhood—defying every statistic placed on her name.

In Search of Love is Sharron's debut poetry collection—an intimate and unapologetic exploration of pain, longing, faith, and healing. Through these pages, she gives voice to the parts of herself once silenced, using poetry as a tool to release, reclaim, and move forward.

With a combination of lived experience, higher education, and a passion for storytelling, Sharron empowers others who've faced adversity to find their own voice. She believes in faith over fear, growth over grief, and purpose over pain.

When she's not engaged in activities with raising her children, Sharron is doing community service, mentoring young people, and working on new entrepreneurial adventures.

You can connect with her on social media or by email to share your story or learn more about upcoming work.